FOCUS ON CURRENT EVENTS

PROTESTS

by Emma Kaiser

THERE IS
NO
PLANET
B

FOCUS
READERS®

VOYAGER

www.focusreaders.com

Focus Readers is distributed by North Star Editions:
sales@northstareditions.com | 888-417-0195

Produced for Focus Readers by Red Line Editorial.

Content Consultant: Deana Rohlinger, PhD, Professor of Sociology, Florida State University

Photographs ©: Shutterstock Images, cover, 1, 4–5, 7, 9, 10–11, 16–17, 19, 27, 29, 33, 37, 39, 41, 42–43, 44; iStockphoto, 13, 34–35; Vecteezy, 15 (fist, armored officers, flag), 15 (phone); Red Line Editorial, 21; Atlanta Journal-Constitution/AP Images, 22–23; AP Images, 25; Charles Knoblock/AP Images, 30–31

Library of Congress Cataloging-in-Publication Data
Library of Congress Cataloging-in-Publication Data is available on the Library of Congress website.

ISBN
978-1-63739-079-5 (hardcover)
978-1-63739-133-4 (paperback)
978-1-63739-234-8 (ebook pdf)
978-1-63739-187-7 (hosted ebook)

Printed in the United States of America
Mankato, MN
012022

ABOUT THE AUTHOR

Emma Kaiser is a writer and educator based in Saint Paul, Minnesota. She has an MFA in Creative Writing from the University of Minnesota, and her writing has been published in a number of magazines and publications. She is the author of two other nonfiction books for students.

TABLE OF CONTENTS

CHAPTER 1

THE START OF A MOVEMENT

On May 25, 2020, police officers in Minneapolis, Minnesota, arrested a Black man named George Floyd. He had allegedly tried to use a fake $20 bill. A video of the arrest was recorded and posted online. It showed officer Derek Chauvin, a white man, kneeling on the back of George Floyd's neck for 9 minutes and 29 seconds. Floyd was handcuffed and repeatedly said, "I can't breathe." Chauvin did not get off

The area around Cup Foods, where George Floyd was killed, was made into a memorial.

Floyd's neck. Floyd was later pronounced dead. The video went viral.

The next day, crowds began to gather outside the Third Precinct police station in Minneapolis. People filled the streets with signs that read "Black Lives Matter" and "Justice for George Floyd." Crowds chanted Floyd's last words: "I can't breathe." Thousands marched through the streets of Minneapolis. Because of the COVID-19 virus that spread around the world in 2020, people had been inside and distant from one another for more than two months. But they could not be kept inside any longer. They were there to protest George Floyd's death.

For years, people had been protesting unfair treatment of Black people, especially Black men, at the hands of law enforcement. Studies found that Black people are more likely to be killed than

⚐ Some protesters carried signs with the names of Black people who had been killed, some by police officers.

white people in their interactions with police. Several of these deaths gained national attention. In 2014, Michael Brown was shot by police in Ferguson, Missouri. In 2016, Philando Castile was shot by police during a traffic stop in Falcon Heights, Minnesota. In March 2020, Breonna Taylor was shot by police as they raided her apartment in Louisville, Kentucky. People were upset by this pattern of police violence against people of color. They wanted to see change.

In the week after George Floyd's death, millions of people gathered in protests across the United States. By June 1, protests over racial injustice were taking place in countries all around the world. A global movement had begun.

A few protests turned into riots where people looted stores or burned buildings. However, most of the protests remained peaceful. Police responded to numerous protests with tear gas and rubber bullets. Hundreds of protesters were injured. But they continued to gather and call for change.

And change did happen. State and federal governments worked on creating laws focused on police reform. Cities looked for ways to improve relationships between police and people of color.

Protesters gather in Manchester, England, in June 2020 to show their support for the Black Lives Matter movement.

Chauvin was charged with murder and manslaughter. He was found guilty and sentenced to prison. But the change didn't stop there. The protest movement motivated people to fight racial injustice in other areas, too. For example, some companies committed to making their workplaces more **inclusive**. By coming together, people found a way to make their voices heard.

CHAPTER 2

THE POWER OF PROTESTS

A protest is a public objection to an action, system, or idea. Protests can take many forms. A protest can be an individual resisting. Or it can be a mass demonstration. Usually, protests involve a group of people expressing an opinion and calling for change. Activists often use protests to bring attention to important issues. For this reason, protests have been a key tool in many social movements.

Protesters often participate in marches. These large gatherings show leaders that many people care about an issue.

Throughout history, people have often used protests to call for changes in their governments. People can protest actions or policies they believe are wrong or unfair. Protesting shows people care about an issue, and it pressures leaders to act.

For example, in the 1760s, many American colonists disagreed with how the British ruled them. Taxes were a key issue. Americans paid taxes to the British government on certain items. These included tea, paint, paper, stamps, and glass. However, colonists could not vote or hold office in Great Britain's government. Colonists didn't have a say in the choices Great Britain made or how the government used their tax money. So, many colonists felt the taxes were unfair. To protest, they organized **boycotts**. They refused to buy the taxed items. This hurt the British financially. In response, the British

At the Boston Tea Party, colonists disguised themselves as American Indians while they destroyed British tea.

government ended many of the taxes. But it kept the tax on tea.

To many colonists, this tea tax was a symbol of Great Britain's power over the colonies. To protest, some colonists boarded British tea ships in the middle of the night on December 16, 1773. They dumped hundreds of chests of tea into Boston Harbor. This event became known as the Boston Tea Party. It was one of the events that led to the American Revolutionary War (1775–1783).

The colonies won the war and gained independence. They formed a new country, the United States of America. The US Constitution described how the new country's government would work. It also listed rights the country's **citizens** would have. These rights included the right to speak freely. The Constitution also said people had the right to assemble. That meant they could gather peacefully in groups. These groups often asked the government to make changes.

When the Constitution became law in the 1780s, several of these rights were available to white men only. But over time, more people were included. Protests and the social movements they helped create played a key role in these changes. Today, every US citizen has the right to protest peacefully.

PROTESTING RIGHTS ◄

In the United States, all citizens have certain rights related to protesting.

1. The government may not restrict your speech on private property if you are protesting with the permission of the property owner.

2. Protesters and counterprotesters have the right to free speech, and police must treat both groups equally.

3. When lawfully present in any public space, it is your right to photograph or record anything in plain view, including police.

4. No permit is necessary to march on public sidewalks, as long as car and pedestrian traffic is not obstructed.

CHAPTER 3

PROTESTING FOR REPRESENTATION

P rotests can provide a voice to groups of people who might otherwise be silenced. For example, when the United States was founded, only white men who owned land could vote. States often denied people the right to vote because of race, gender, or religion. This meant that only certain people could participate in the US government. This small portion of people controlled the laws. For decades, women and people of color protested

Many protests focus on protecting the rights of immigrants or other marginalized groups.

these policies. They said they should have the right to vote, too.

The women's **suffrage** movement launched in the 1800s. Members were known as suffragists. They wrote newspapers and articles that criticized laws they saw as unfair. They called on the government to change. Suffragists also used many methods of protesting, including public gatherings and speeches. By educating others, these protests helped the movement gain attention. More people began to call for change.

Suffragists sometimes teamed up with abolitionists, or people who wanted to end slavery. Their efforts helped lead to the Thirteenth Amendment, which abolished slavery after the US Civil War (1861–1865).

A few years later, the Fourteenth and Fifteenth Amendments passed. The Fourteenth Amendment

△ Despite years of protesting, women in the United States couldn't vote in national elections until 1920.

said that anyone born in the United States was a citizen and that all citizens should have equal rights and equal protection. The Fifteenth Amendment specifically said states couldn't prevent citizens from voting because of their race. However, some states found other ways to prevent Black people from voting.

Plus, the Fourteenth Amendment's wording protected voting rights for male citizens only. Many women were still unable to vote. In the 1870s and 1880s, the US government declared that American Indians and some Asian Americans couldn't be citizens. That meant they couldn't vote, either.

By the 1910s, suffragists' methods became more direct. Women's suffrage groups began organizing parades through major US cities. They marched in groups and carried signs. They also picketed outside the White House. Groups of women formed a line and held signs calling for women's suffrage. They wanted to draw attention to their cause and pressure the government to act. Many women were harassed. Many more were unfairly arrested for blocking sidewalks. But the suffrage movement wasn't stopped. In fact, the arrests and protests helped it gain support.

By the early 1900s, several states allowed women to vote. And in 1920, the Nineteenth Amendment took effect. It gave all women the right to vote. However, many people of color were still barred from voting. Later changes granted citizenship to American Indians and Asian Americans. But the fight for equal treatment was far from over.

US CITIZENSHIP TIMELINE ◁

The rights and opportunities available to Americans have changed over time.

The US Constitution allows states to choose who can vote. In most states, this is white, land-owning men.

The Thirteenth Amendment ends slavery in the United States.

The Fifteenth Amendment says states cannot deny citizens the right to vote based on race.

The US Supreme Court rules that American Indians aren't citizens and can't vote.

The Indian Citizenship Act grants citizenship to American Indians, though some states' laws prevent them from voting.

The Twenty-Sixth Amendment lowers the voting age from 21 to 18.

| 1789 | 1828 | 1865 | 1868 | 1870 | 1882 | 1884 | 1920 | 1924 | 1943 | 1971 |

By the presidential election this year, most states had made changes so men were no longer required to own property to vote.

As a result of the Fourteenth Amendment, all men born in the United States are considered citizens and can therefore vote.

The Chinese Exclusion Act bans foreign-born Chinese Americans from voting or becoming citizens.

The Nineteenth Amendment grants women the right to vote. Some states had already made this change in the late 1800s and early 1900s.

The Magnuson Act grants Chinese Americans citizenship and the right to vote.

CHAPTER 4

PROTESTING FOR CIVIL RIGHTS

People often use protests to speak out when their rights are not acknowledged. Protests can put pressure on the government not only to change laws but to enforce them. For example, the Fourteenth and Fifteenth Amendments said all US citizens should have equal rights and equal protection under the law. However, Black Americans continued to face many forms of **discrimination**.

Throughout the 1900s, many protesters called for an end to segregation and racial inequality.

After the Civil War, many states created laws that promoted **segregation**. Black people were required to use separate restaurants, stores, and bathrooms. In several states, unfair literacy tests and expensive poll taxes prevented many Black people from voting. So did white supremacist groups. Black people often risked being attacked or killed if they tried to vote.

People used protests to call attention to these problems. They showed that segregation went against the Constitution. They called for the government to protect the civil rights of Black Americans. Throughout the 1950s and 1960s, a wave of protests swept the United States. The protests took a variety of forms. Many involved civil disobedience, or the deliberate breaking of unfair laws. Protesters stayed peaceful, even if violence was used against them.

▲ Students hold a sit-in to protest at a lunch counter in Portsmouth, Virginia, in February 1960.

For example, people often held sit-ins. One famous sit-in happened in 1960. Four young Black men sat at a lunch counter in North Carolina. They sat in seats reserved for white people. When the waiter refused to serve them, the men refused to leave. They remained seated until the counter closed. Then they returned the next day with more students. This type of protest spread all around the country. The sit-ins brought national attention to the civil rights movement. They also led to businesses finally **integrating**.

Another famous event was the March on Washington. On August 28, 1963, approximately 250,000 people of all races gathered in the nation's capital. There, Martin Luther King Jr. gave his famous "I Have a Dream" speech. He called for equal rights and opportunities for all people.

The work of these protesters and activists led to some key legal changes. The Supreme Court declared segregation unconstitutional. President Lyndon B. Johnson signed several new laws. The Civil Rights Act supported integration and equal

➤ THINK ABOUT IT

Can you think of examples of people who protest discrimination today?

At the March on Washington, people called for new laws to protect the rights of people of color.

employment. The Voting Rights Act helped end poll taxes and unfair literacy tests. And the Fair Housing Act banned housing discrimination.

However, these changes came at a cost. Thousands of protesters faced violence or were arrested. Some, including Martin Luther King Jr., were killed. And in many areas of life, inequity continued. Work to end discrimination is ongoing.

THE MONTGOMERY BUS BOYCOTT

The Montgomery Bus Boycott played a key role in the civil rights movement. Before the boycott, buses in Montgomery, Alabama, were segregated. Black riders had to sit in a separate section in the back. But white riders could take these seats if the front section was full.

The boycott began on December 5, 1955. A few days earlier, Rosa Parks had been arrested for not giving up her seat on a bus. She was part of the NAACP, a group focused on ending racial discrimination. To support this goal, activists called for a one-day boycott of the bus system. More than 40,000 Black people refused to ride the buses. After that, civil rights leaders decided to extend the boycott. People worked together to create carpools. And some taxi drivers reduced

The Montgomery Bus Boycott was the first large-scale protest against segregation in the United States.

their rates. Many people simply walked to their destinations.

The boycott lasted 381 days. Black Americans were the majority of the city's bus riders. So, the bus system lost lots of money. Protesters also filed a lawsuit. The case eventually reached the Supreme Court, which ruled that segregation was unconstitutional. Buses were finally integrated on December 21, 1956. By that time, the boycott and its leaders had received national attention.

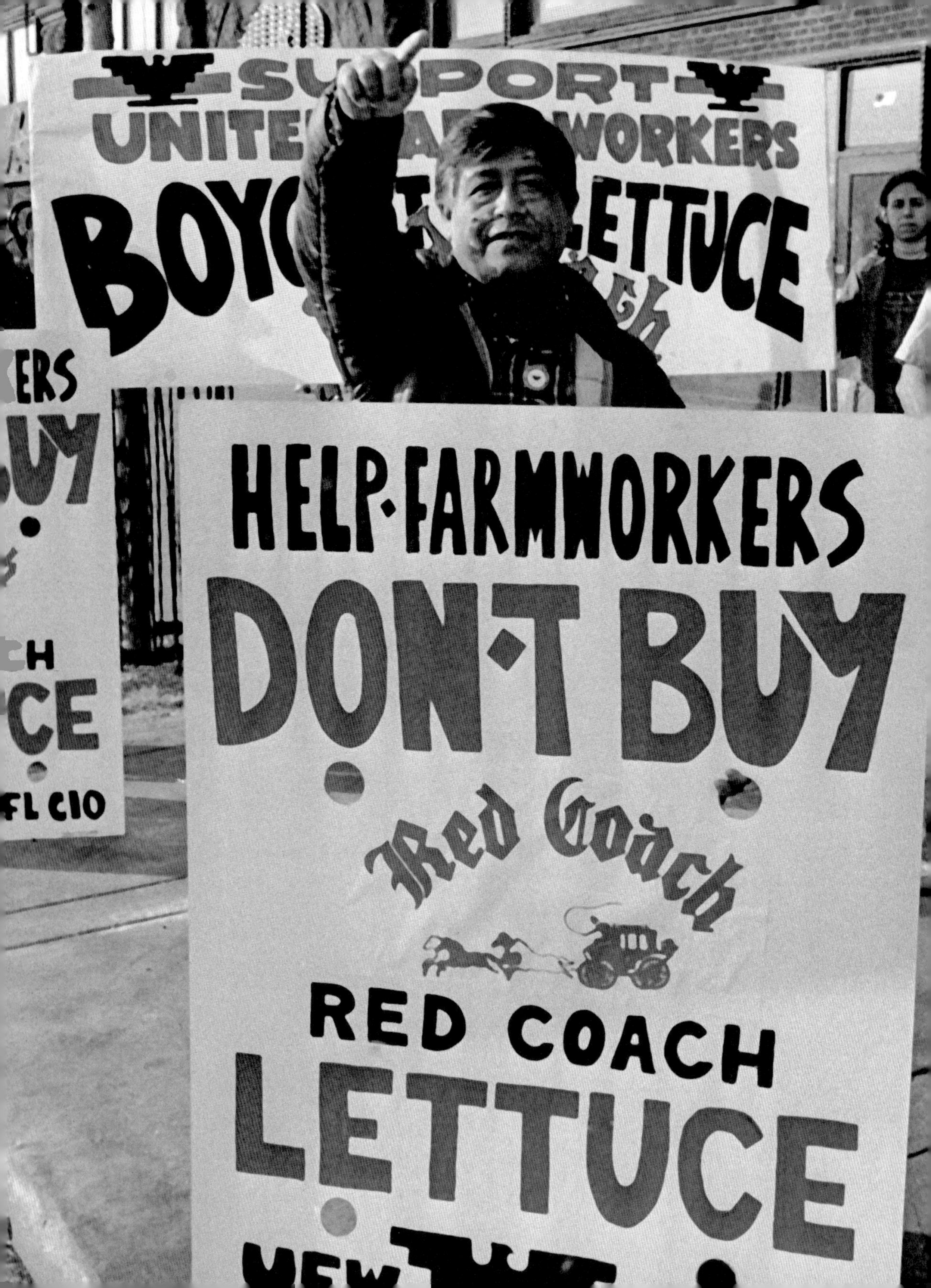
HELP·FARMWORKERS
DON·T BUY
Red Coach
RED COACH
LETTUCE

CHAPTER 5

PROTESTING FOR WORKERS' RIGHTS

Protesting can shape laws and governments. It can also change policies in business. Through strikes, picketing, and boycotts, workers can protest for better pay and working conditions. One successful example is the Delano Grape Strike. This strike began in California. For decades, Filipino and Mexican immigrants had worked to harvest the region's grapes. However, they received low wages and very poor working

Workers who picked crops used strikes and boycotts to raise attention to problems they faced.

conditions. In 1965, they decided to strike against the Delano-area grape growers. They would not work until they received better working conditions.

The workers asked Cesar Chavez to support them. Chavez was a leader of a **labor union** called the National Farm Workers Association. He agreed to join the strike. His union did, too.

The strike lasted five years. During this time, farm workers encouraged people all over North America to stop buying grapes. This boycott caused grape growers to lose money. Eventually, the growers gave in. They met with workers. They agreed to pay higher wages and provide better working conditions.

Workers use similar methods today. When the COVID-19 pandemic spread around the world in 2020, many people stayed home to avoid

▲ During the COVID-19 pandemic, some workers at companies such as Amazon and Target went on strike.

getting sick. But people with jobs in health care, factories, and stores often still had to go to work. As a result, these workers had a higher risk of getting the virus. Many got sick. On May 1, some workers went on strike. They wanted companies to make changes. They asked for higher pay, more time off, and better protective gear.

Protesting can give workers power to influence their companies. When workers come together, they can often get leaders to do what they ask.

CHAPTER 6

CHALLENGING POWER

People around the world use protests to challenge the **status quo**. For example, the Middle East and North Africa saw a wave of pro-democracy protests in the 2010s. The first took place in Tunisia. People protested poverty and government corruption. The protests turned into an uprising. The country's leader was forced to step down. Then Tunisians held an election. Voters chose a new president. Soon after, protests

Protests in Egypt in 2011 led the country's leader to step down. He had been in power for 30 years.

took place in several surrounding countries. Some led to uprisings or unrest.

Because protests challenge power, they can be seen as threats. Protesters may face arrest or violence. Governments may also try to prevent people from gathering.

One example took place in Hong Kong. Hong Kong has a different system of government than the rest of China. But in 2019, leaders announced plans for a law that would allow people to be tried for crimes in mainland China instead of courts in Hong Kong. Many Hong Kong residents feared the new law would limit their rights. Huge groups of protesters gathered in the city's streets. They were often met with force. Thousands of protesters were arrested or injured by police.

Plans for the law were dropped in fall 2019. But the protests sparked a pro-democracy movement.

Hundreds of thousands of protesters filled the streets of Hong Kong on June 9, 2019.

Marches continued throughout 2020, even when marching was declared illegal.

People in Hong Kong need permits to gather publicly. The government tried to stop protests by not granting these permits. In addition, a national security law passed in 2020. Many people worried it would limit freedom of speech and assembly.

The public response to protests can vary, too. Protesters may be described as violent. They may be accused of trying to stir up trouble. It's true that some protests can be disruptive. Some protests block roads or traffic. And some involve breaking the law or damage to property. However, claims that protesters are violent can be a way to discredit them. These claims aren't always true. But they still shape how people see the protests.

The response to protesters can also depend on who is protesting. In 2020, many Black Lives Matter protests took place. One peaceful protest outside the White House was met with armed police in riot gear. The police dispersed protesters with tear gas. In 2021, crowds of mostly white people protested Donald Trump's election loss to Joe Biden. They broke through barriers, assaulted police officers, and overtook the US Capitol. It took law enforcement hours to regain control and remove them. Many commentators argued that

Police officers sometimes wear riot gear for protection when responding to protests.

this reaction would have been very different if the protesters had been people of color.

Around the world, people use protesting as a way to challenge systems of power. They speak out, even if it means risking their lives. Protests can be controversial. But they can also pressure leaders to make changes.

THE DAKOTA ACCESS PIPELINE

In 2016, lawmakers approved construction of the Dakota Access Pipeline. This pipeline would carry oil from North Dakota to Illinois. However, it would run through sacred land belonging to the Standing Rock Sioux Tribe. Members of this tribe said it would disrupt their burial grounds. It would also run close to a local reservation. The tribe said this violated federal law and treaties with the Sioux. People also worried the pipeline would pollute the Missouri River if it leaked.

Thousands of protesters began gathering in North Dakota. They came to oppose the pipeline. Many protesters faced an armed police force. The police came with tanks and riot gear. They used tear gas and rubber bullets on protesters. Hundreds of protesters were arrested. Some

Thousands of protesters stayed in camps near the Missouri River to oppose the Dakota Access Pipeline.

were zapped with Tasers. Police were accused of excessive force.

The fate of the pipeline remained unresolved for years. Legal challenges led to a judge revoking the permit to build it. The judge also called for an environmental assessment.

Further, the protesters drew national attention to issues of Indigenous rights. They called for treaties to be upheld. And they raised concern about protecting the environment. Their protests inspired thousands of people to take action.

CHAPTER 7

YOUNG PEOPLE AND PROTESTING

People must be a certain age to vote or run for office. But no one is too young to protest. In fact, students played a huge role in the civil rights movement. Young people continue taking to the streets today. They use their voices for causes they believe in. Protests can raise awareness about important issues. Often, these issues affect young people directly. In 2018, survivors of a school shooting in Parkland, Florida, organized

At a March For Our Lives protest, students speak out against gun violence and school shootings.

▲ Greta Thunberg skipped school to protest. She held a sign calling for action on climate change.

a march to protest gun violence and demand stricter gun-control laws. Thousands of people attended. Hundreds of similar marches took place across the United States and around the world.

Protests give young people a way to call their leaders to action. For example, Swedish teenager Greta Thunberg thought her country wasn't doing enough to stop climate change. So, in 2018, she began a school strike. She encouraged others to join her. Within a few months, thousands of students held similar strikes around the world. In 2019, Greta spoke at an international climate conference. She urged world leaders to act. She asked them to cut carbon **emissions** and invest in **sustainable** technologies. Her activism inspired millions of people.

These students are proof of how people can work together to make changes. By taking a stand for what they believe in, people can impact their communities, their country, and the world.

THINK ABOUT IT ◁

What issues are important to you? How could you raise awareness about them?

FOCUS ON
PROTESTS

Write your answers on a separate piece of paper.

1. Write a paragraph describing one protest from the civil rights movement and the change it helped create.

2. Do you find it easy or hard to speak up about causes you believe in? Why do you think that is?

3. Which type of protests involve people refusing to work as a way to call for change?

> **A.** boycott
> **B.** picketing
> **C.** strike

4. Why might a country's government try to limit people's right to protest?

> **A.** The government might want to give people more freedom.
> **B.** The government might want to hear new ideas.
> **C.** The government might not want to make changes.

Answer key on page 48.

GLOSSARY

boycotts
Protests in which people refuse to buy certain goods or services.

citizens
People who live in or come from a certain country and have specific rights as a result.

discrimination
Unfair treatment of a person or group based on race, gender, or other factors.

emissions
Chemicals or substances that are released into the air, especially ones that harm the environment.

inclusive
Having equal treatment and opportunities for all kinds of people.

integrating
Ending a policy of segregation.

labor union
An organization that protects the rights of workers.

segregation
The separation of groups of people based on race or other factors.

status quo
The way things are currently.

suffrage
The right to vote.

sustainable
Having to do with methods that do not harm or use up a resource.

TO LEARN MORE

BOOKS

Braun, Eric. *Protest Movements: Then and Now*. North Mankato, MN: Capstone Press, 2018.

Harris, Duchess, and Kate Conley. *Citizenship, Race, and the Law*. Minneapolis: Abdo Publishing, 2020.

MacCarald, Clara. *The Standing Rock Sioux Challenge the Dakota Access Pipeline*. Lake Elmo, MN: Focus Readers, 2019.

NOTE TO EDUCATORS

Visit **www.focusreaders.com** to find lesson plans, activities, links, and other resources related to this title.

INDEX